CHART HITS FOR TWO

Arrangements by Peter Deneff

ISBN 978-1-70516-832-5

Visit Hal Leonard Online at
www.halleonard.com

World headquarters, contact:
Hal Leonard
7777 West Bluemound Road
Milwaukee, WI 53213
Email: info@halleonard.com

In Europe contact:
Hal Leonard Europe Limited
1 Red Place
London, W1K 6PL
Email: info@halleonardeurope.com

In Australia contact:
Hal Leonard Australia Pty. Ltd.
4 Lentara Court
Cheltenham, Victoria, 3192 Australia
Email: info@halleonard.com.au

ALL TOO WELL

ALTO SAXES

Words and Music by TAYLOR SWIFT
and LIZ ROSE

Moderately

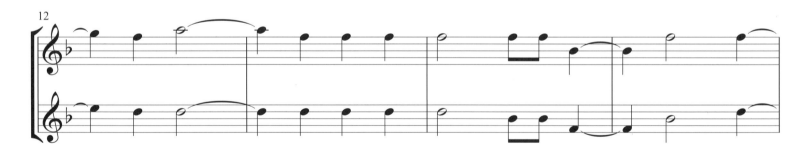

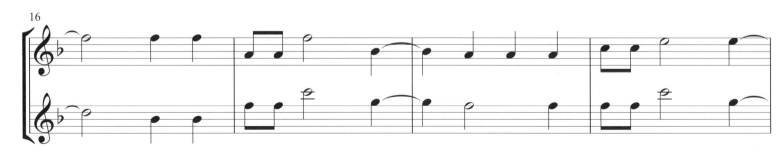

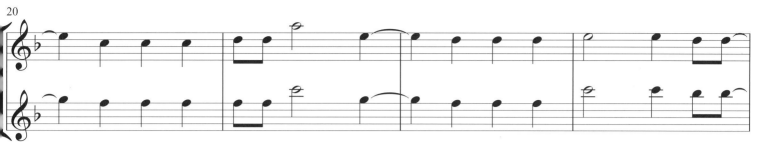

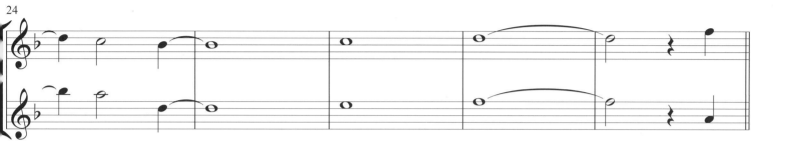

BAD HABITS

ALTO SAXES

Words and Music by ED SHEERAN,
JOHNNY McDAID and FRED GIBSON

Upbeat Pop

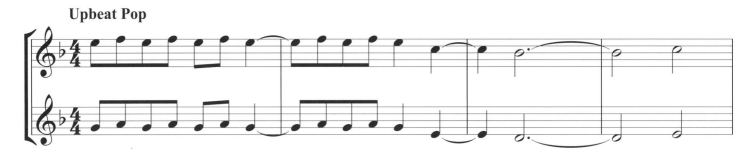

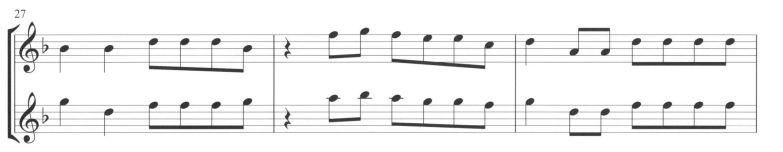

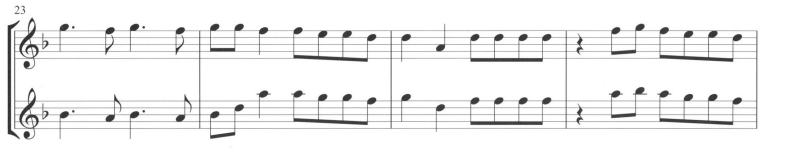

BANG!

ALTO SAXES

Words and Music by ADAM METZGER,
JACK METZGER and RYAN METZGER

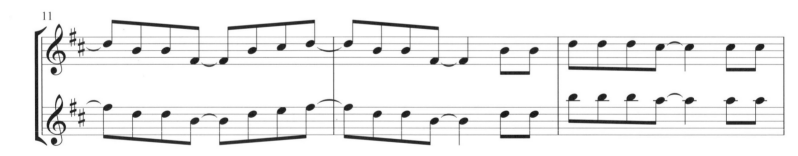

BELIEVER

ALTO SAXES

Words and Music by DAN REYNOLDS,
WAYNE SERMON, BEN McKEE,
DANIEL PLATZMAN, JUSTIN TRANTOR,
MATTIAS LARSSON and ROBIN FREDRICKSSON

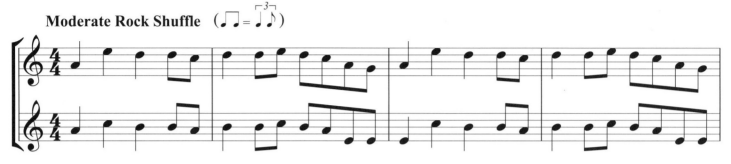

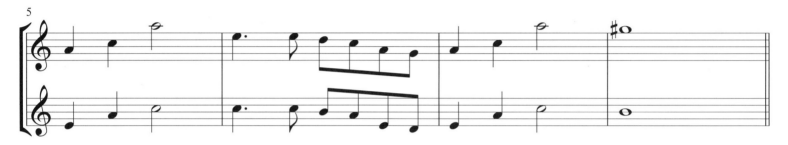

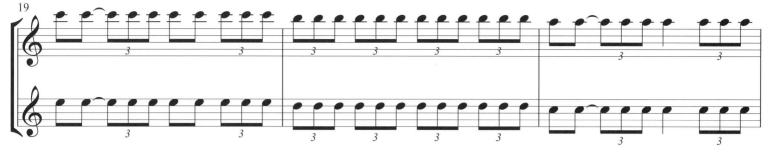

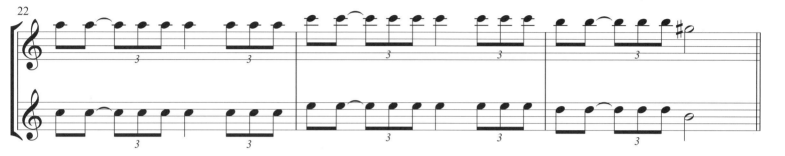

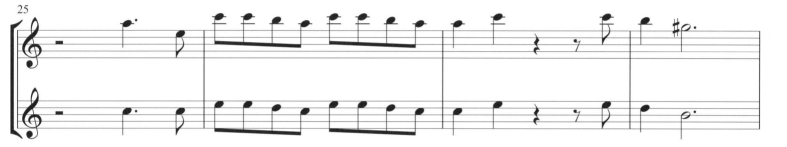

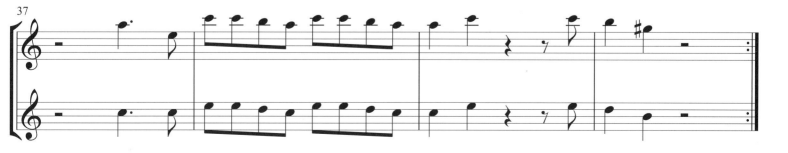

BLINDING LIGHTS

ALTO SAXES

Words and Music by ABEL TESFAYE,
MAX MARTIN, JASON QUENNEVILLE,
OSCAR HOLTER and AHMAD BALSHE

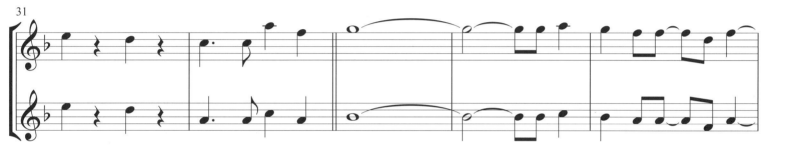

DESPACITO

ALTO SAXES

Words and Music by LUIS FONSI,
ERIKA ENDER, JUSTIN BIEBER, JASON BOYD,
MARTY JAMES GARTON and RAMÓN AYALA

Moderately, in 2

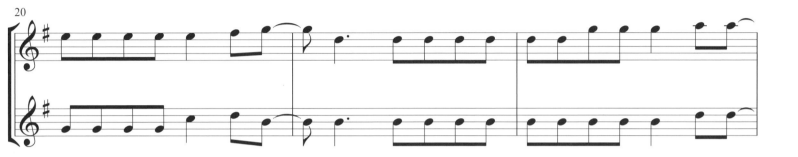

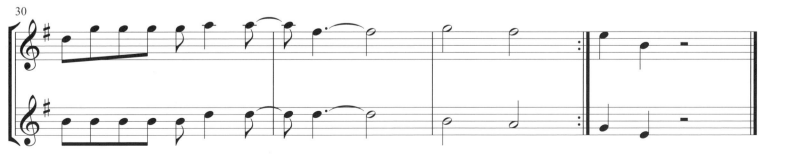

DRIVERS LICENSE

ALTO SAXES

Words and Music by OLIVIA RODRIGO
and DANIEL NIGRO

Moderately slow

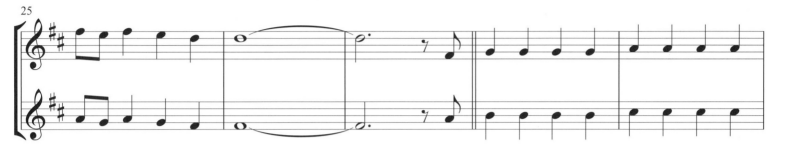

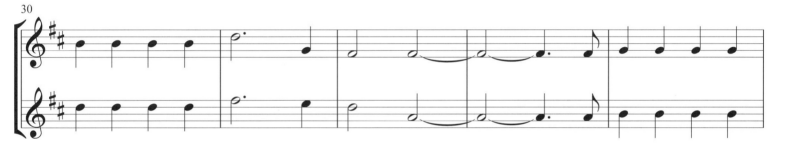

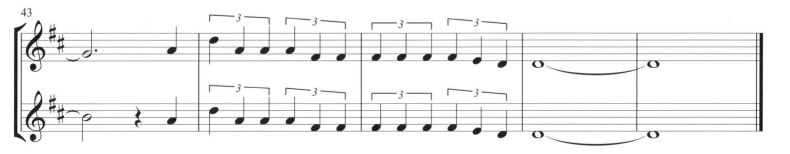

DYNAMITE

ALTO SAXES

Words and Music by JESSICA AGOMBAR
and DAVID STEWART

Moderately fast

EASY ON ME

ALTO SAXES

Words and Music by ADELE ADKINS
and GREG KURSTIN

Moderate Ballad

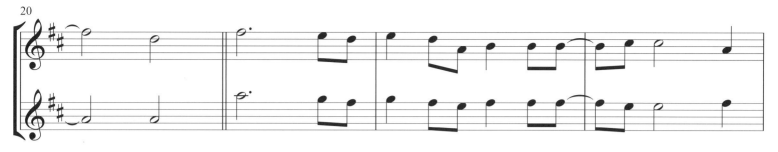

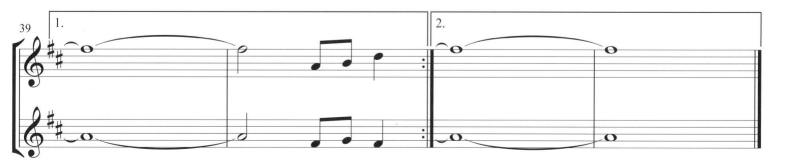

HAPPIER THAN EVER

ALTO SAXES

Words and Music by BILLIE EILISH O'CONNELL
and FINNEAS O'CONNELL

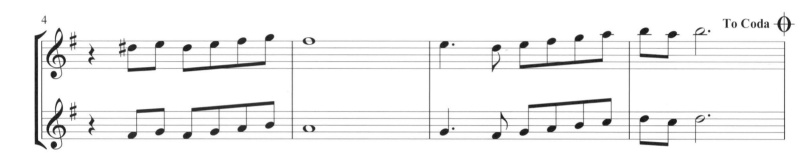

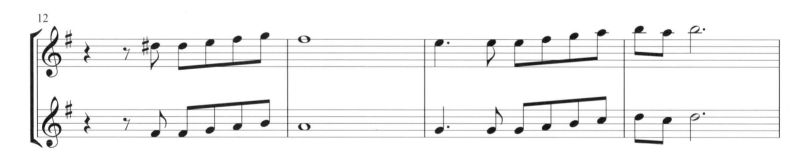

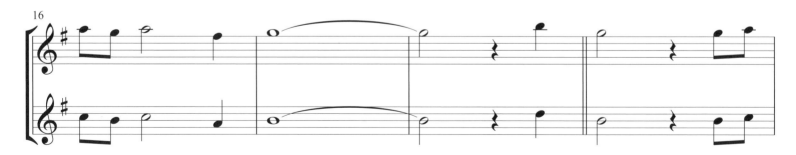

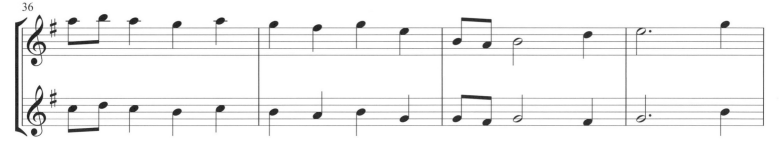

D.S. al Coda

CODA

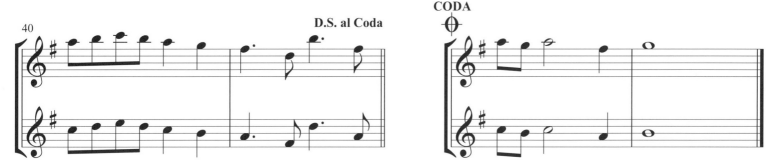

HAVANA

ALTO SAXES

Words and Music by CAMILA CABELLO, LOUIS BELL,
PHARRELL WILLIAMS, ADAM FEENEY, ALI TAMPOSI,
JEFFERY LAMAR WILLIAMS, BRIAN LEE, ANDREW WOTMAN,
BRITTANY HAZZARD and KAAN GUNESBERK

Moderately

HEAT WAVES

ALTO SAXES

Words and Music by
DAVE BAYLEY

Moderate Pop

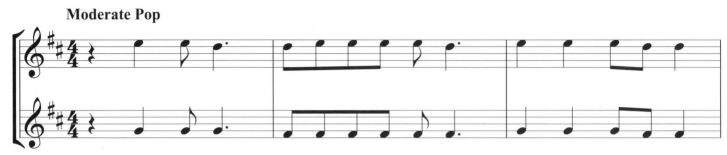

D.S. al Coda

CODA

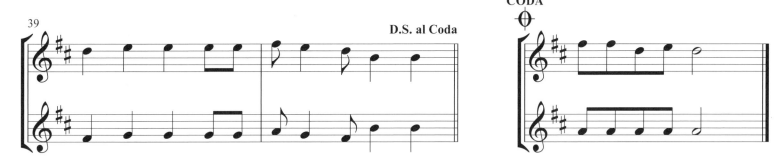

HIGH HOPES

ALTO SAXES

Words and Music by BRENDON URIE,
WILLIAM LOBBAN BEAN, JONAS JEBERG,
SAMUEL HOLLANDER, JACOB SINCLAIR,
JENNY OWEN YOUNGS, ILSEY JUBER,
LAUREN PRITCHARD and TAYLA PARX

D.S. al Fine

LOOK WHAT YOU MADE ME DO

ALTO SAXES

Words and Music by TAYLOR SWIFT,
JACK ANTONOFF, RICHARD FAIRBRASS,
FRED FAIRBRASS and ROB MANZOLI

Moderately fast

MILLION REASONS

ALTO SAXES

Words and Music by STEFANI GERMANOTTA,
MARK RONSON and HILLARY LINDSEY

NO TIME TO DIE

from NO TIME TO DIE

ALTO SAXES

Words and Music by BILLIE EILISH O'CONNELL
and FINNEAS O'CONNELL

Moderately

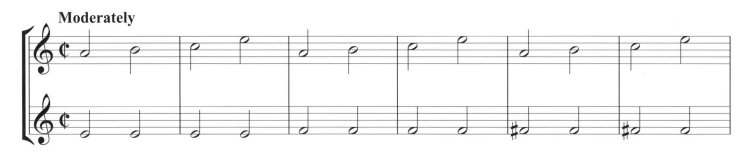

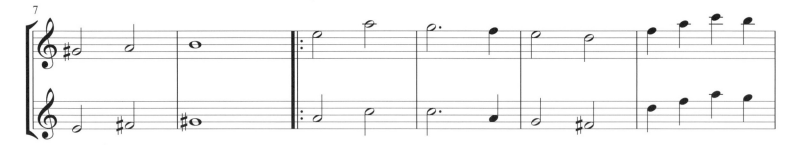

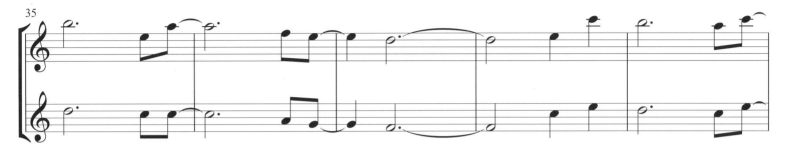

PERFECT

ALTO SAXES

Words and Music by
ED SHEERAN

Classic Ballad

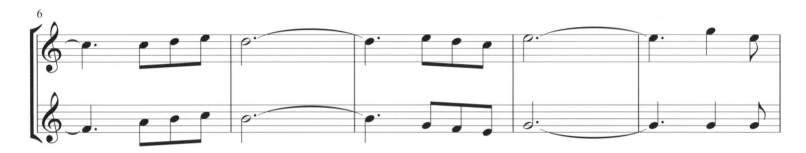

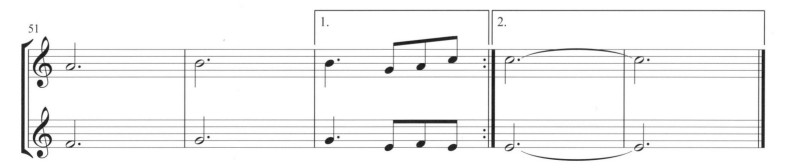

PERMISSION TO DANCE

ALTO SAXES

Words and Music by ED SHEERAN,
JOHNNY McDAID, STEVE MAC
and JENNA ANDREWS

Bright Dance beat

SEÑORITA

ALTO SAXES

Words and Music by CAMILA CABELLO,
CHARLOTTE AITCHISON, JACK PATTERSON,
SHAWN MENDES, MAGNUS HØIBERG,
BENJAMIN LEVIN, ALI TAMPOSI
and ANDREW WOTMAN

Moderate Latin groove

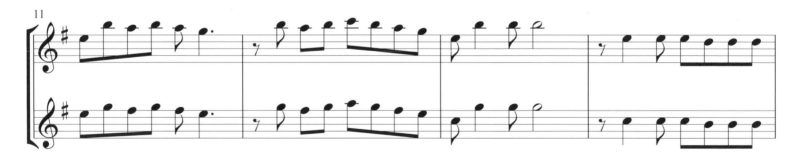

SHALLOW
from A STAR IS BORN

ALTO SAXES

Words and Music by STEFANI GERMANOTTA,
MARK RONSON, ANDREW WYATT
and ANTHONY ROSSOMANDO

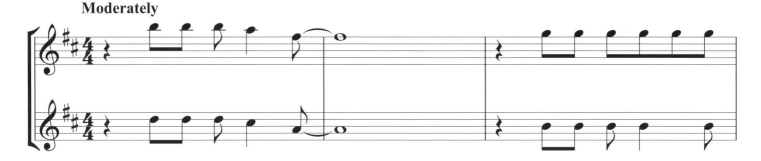

SURFACE PRESSURE

from ENCANTO

ALTO SAXES

Music and Lyrics by
LIN-MANUEL MIRANDA

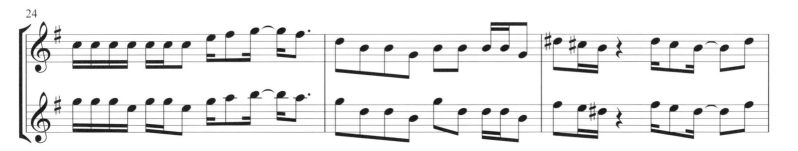

TOO GOOD AT GOODBYES

ALTO SAXES

Words and Music by SAM SMITH,
TOR HERMANSEN, MIKKEL ERIKSEN
and JAMES NAPIER

Pop Ballad

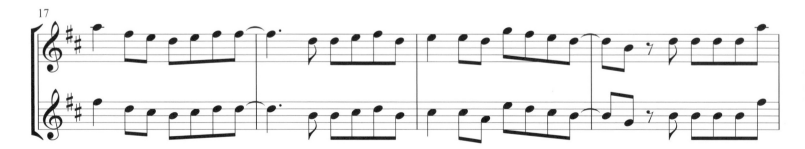

WE DON'T TALK ABOUT BRUNO

from ENCANTO

ALTO SAXES

Music and Lyrics by
LIN-MANUEL MIRANDA

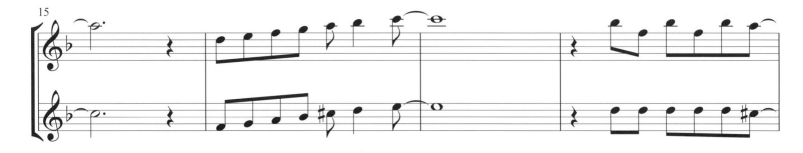

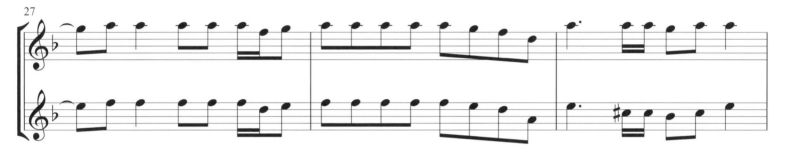

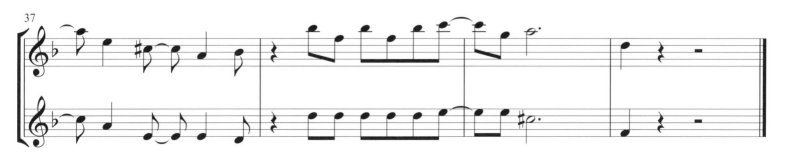